What I lick
before
Your face

What I lick before Your face

and other haikus by dogs

Jamie Coleman

BANTAM PRESS

LONDON · NEW YORK · TORONTO · SYDNEY · AUCKLAND

TRANSWORLD PUBLISHERS
61–63 Uxbridge Road, London W5 5SA
www.penguin.co.uk

Transworld is part of the Penguin Random House group of companies
whose addresses can be found at global.penguinrandomhouse.com

First published in Great Britain in 2018 by Bantam Press
an imprint of Transworld Publishers

A CIP catalogue record for this book
is available from the British Library.

ISBN 9781787631144

Designed and typeset in Sabon LT Std by Bobby Birchall, Bobby&Co.
Printed and bound in Italy by Printer Trento s.r.l.

All images © Shutterstock, apart from page 128 which is supplied courtesy
of the author

Penguin Random House is committed to a sustainable
future for our business, our readers and our planet. This book
is made from Forest Stewardship Council® certified paper.

5 7 9 10 8 6 4

haiku /ˈhʌɪkuː/ ▶ n. (pl. same or **haikus**) a Japanese poem of seventeen syllables, in three lines of five, seven, and five.

dog /ˈdɒg/ ▶ n. poet

Homework

I don't know that word
But I'm completely certain
I didn't eat it

The Throne

The water you keep
In the dog-height chair, you say
It's NOT for drinking?

Grass

Why do I eat grass?
Perhaps today is the day
It is sausages

Going to the Park

Forgive my distrust
But last time you said 'the park'
Someone took my balls

Best Friend

The definition
Of friendship must surely be
You, a bag, my poo

Returning

Whenever you leave
The wonder of your return
Almost makes things whole

The Boss

I just eat and sleep
And you collect my faeces
But sure you're the boss

The Roll

That paper you keep
In a roll, next to the seat
I fixed that for you

Rubs

It hurts my feelings
When you avoid stroking there
Nipples are me too

Playing

I do not believe
That your fixation with my
Playing dead is fine

When I Look Up at You

You think that we think
You are perfect creations
We know you need that

Standing

I sometimes feel bad
That I don't get as happy
Whenever you sit

Joy

Although it is true
That I enjoy balls and bones
They don't define me

Bed

Before sleep, we turn
Circling again and again
This disappearing

What's That, Boy?

When you look like that
Sometimes, it's like you're trying
To tell me something

Perfection

It is so perfect
That the warm small of your back
Fits my cold nose so

The Tail That Wags

Sometimes I'm happy
But often it's a little
More complicated

What I Lick Before Your Face

You may take my balls
But I will lick what remains
And then, dear, your face

Who's a Good Boy

I no longer know
If you're being genuine
Or rhetorical

A Better Boy

Yes, good is OK
But I want to be better
Perhaps a great boy?

Panting

You try keeping cool
When the only hairless bit
Is inside your mouth

Chair

We should have a talk
About the chair. No biggie
I'm fine with sharing

Nappies

Now that they have bred
They keep parcels of faeces
For me to open

The Ball

I bring you the ball
You throw it far, far away
Summer follows spring

Slippers

My advice to you
Is have one set of foot things
Then I can relax

The Smell of All Things

If I didn't check
Who knows how the world might smell?
Yes, mainly dog wee

Pats

You seem to believe
That I like being patted
I prefer bacon

Front Legs

There's no easy way
For me to break this to you
Your front legs are weird

The Lead

You make me bring you
This harness of oppression
In my own damn mouth

Doggy Style

How would you like it
If I reduced your species
To sex logistics

Selfish

Hey, would it kill you,
Every once in a while,
To lick my face back?

Going to Live on the Farm

Guys, there is no farm
I wish there was, but there is
Only nothingness

Dog Farts

How about you try
Eating what you make me eat
Before you judge me

Conspiracy

This whole 'cat, dog thing'
Is entirely happening
On television

Perspective

To be fair, although
I have made rather a mess
You steal testicles

The Door Hole

If I didn't bark
Who knows what terrible things
Might come through the hole

Your Things

You keep throwing it
I keep on bringing it back
Look. After. Your. Things.

Walkies

I have come to loathe
That singsong voice you employ
It demeans us both

Beg

What kind of a man
Will only feed their best friend
If they beg for it?

The Moving Thing

Nobody knows what
Happens if I don't do this
But let's not risk it

Shoes

How about next time
You don't make foot coverings
From delicious cow?

Howl

I saw the best minds
Of my generation, lick
Each other's bumholes

A Balanced Diet

To be honest, dear
We find it a little odd
That you don't eat poop

A Dog's Life

Your use of this phrase
Shows a striking ignorance
Of what makes life nice

Toilet

I have a complaint
Someone keeps leaving huge poos
In my special bowl

Names

Within me there lies
The blood of a million wolves
You named me 'Fluffy'

Buried

Last night, I buried
The thing I adore the most
Can you get it please?

The Table

If I just sit here,
Contemplating nothingness
Sausages might come?

Beware

Think how you would feel
If there was a sign saying
'Beware the human'

Al Fresco

Lunch, no longer lunch
Pooling in autumn sunshine
Becomes again lunch

Good Boy

Your predilection
For giving this constant praise
Says more about you

The Outside Bell

It is very rude
That you don't call out in joy
When people arrive

After the Puddle

We can both agree
That the only solution
Is violent shaking

An Offering

I do not have much
But what little that I do
I place in your shoes

Licks

You seem to think that
The licking thing signals love
Salt is delicious

Crayons

Oh, kind tiny one,
Who fed me the coloured sticks
Now I poop rainbows

The Past in Front of Us

This tail I follow
Rich with possibilities
Behind us, futures . . .

Shame

Now that you say it
It seems pretty obvious
I shouldn't have peed

White Lies

You throw the ball and
I will chase it, though clearly
It's behind your back

A New Perspective

Life is so puzzling
But perhaps it will make sense
If I tilt my head

A Winter Morning

I have come to think
That neither of us enjoys
These walks. Shall we stop?

Jamie Coleman has been looking deeply into the eyes of dogs for many years. He works in publishing and lives in south London with his wife, son, and a lurcher called Scout. This is his first collection of poetry.